WELCOME TO ISRAEL WITH SESAME STREET

CHRISTY PETERSON

Lerner Publications ◆ Minneapolis

In this series, *Sesame Street* characters help readers learn about other countries' people, cultures, landscapes, and more. These books connect friends around the world while giving readers new tools to become smarter, kinder friends. Pack your bags and take a fun-filled look at your world with your funny, furry friends from *Sesame Street*.

—Sincerely, the Editors at Sesame Street

TABLE OF CONTENTS

WELCOME TO ISRAEL!

Israel is in the Middle East, which is on the continent of Asia. Most people speak Hebrew or Arabic.

Shalom! That means "hello" in Hebrew. My name is Avigail.

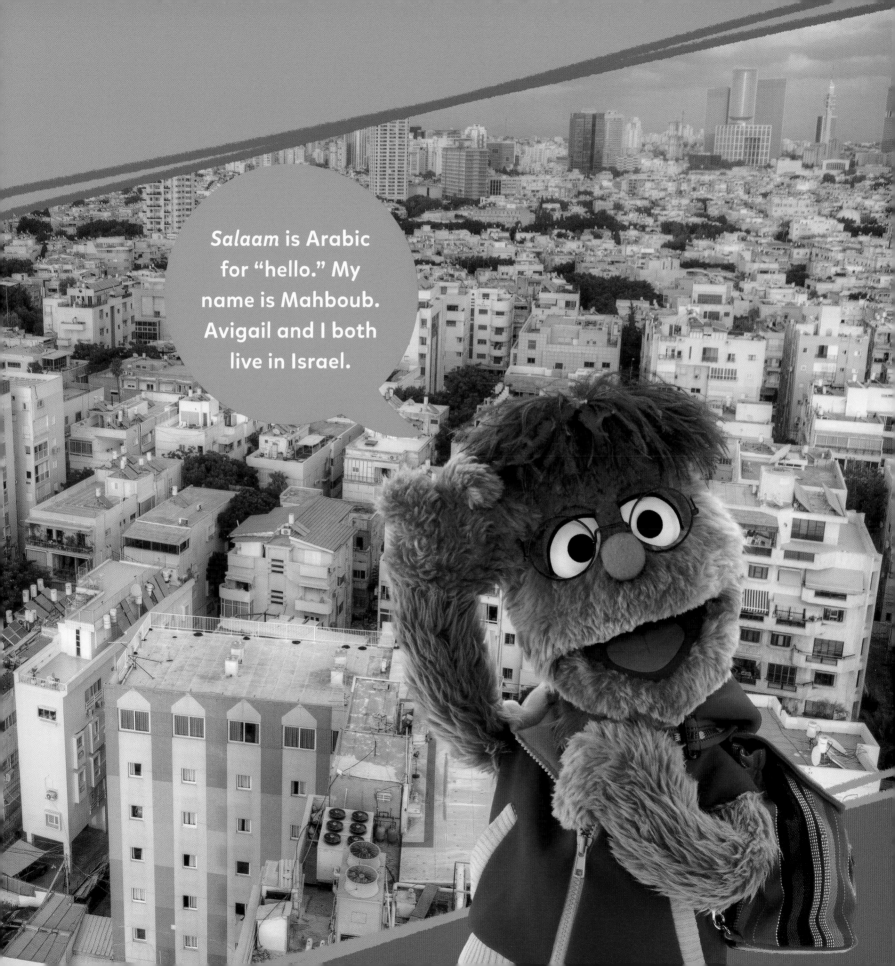

WHERE IN THE WORLD IS ISRAEL?

Israel and Surrounding Area

MEDITERRANEAN SEA

Jordan River

Jerusalem

Dead Sea

ISRAEL

Miles
0   20   40
0   20   40   60
Kilometers

N

NORTH AMERICA

ATLANTIC OCEAN

PACIFIC OCEAN

SOUTH AMERICA

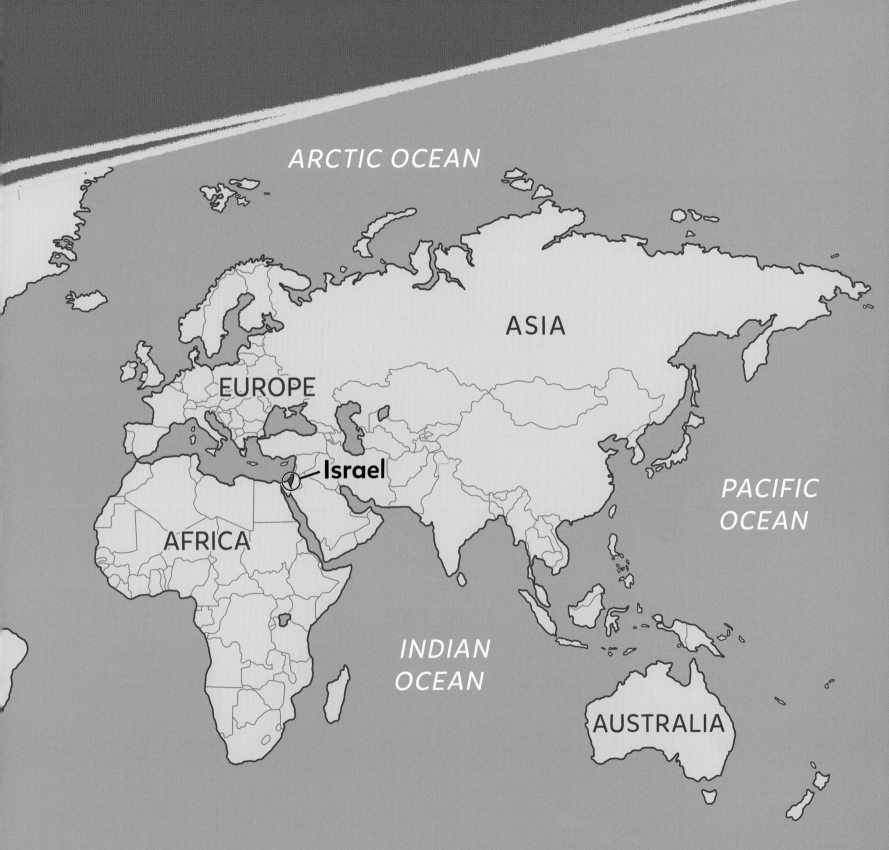

ARCTIC OCEAN

ASIA

EUROPE

Israel

AFRICA

PACIFIC
OCEAN

INDIAN
OCEAN

AUSTRALIA

SOUTHERN OCEAN

Israel has beaches, mountains, and deserts. Summers are hot. Rain often falls in winter.

Most people in Israel live in large cities. Jerusalem is the biggest city.

Jerusalem is a very old city. It is special to people of many religions.

11

Some families live on farms. Farmers in Israel grow many crops. Common crops are avocados and olives.

Jewish people celebrate Rosh Hashanah, the Jewish New Year. They gather with their families and eat special foods.

Falafel is a popular food in Israel. Falafel is a fried ball of chickpeas and herbs.

Markets in Jerusalem have so many different foods to try!

On the first day of school, students have special parties and bring their families to celebrate.

19

Many people visit Israel. They come to see places where people lived long ago. They also come to see modern places.

Flag of Israel

ISRAEL FAST FACTS

Continent: Asia

Largest city: Jerusalem

Population: 9 million

Main languages: Hebrew and Arabic

21

GLOSSARY

celebrate: to throw a party or hold an event to honor a special person or day

crop: a plant that people grow for food or other uses

falafel: a mixture of beans, herbs, and spices that is formed into balls and cooked

market: a place where people buy and sell things

special: something that is different or set apart in some way

LEARN MORE

Ofanansky, Allison. *Tisha B'Av: A Jerusalem Journey.*
Minneapolis: Kar-Ben Publishing, 2017.

Press, J. P. *Welcome to Arabic with Sesame Street.*
Minneapolis: Lerner Publications, 2020.

Press, J. P. *Welcome to Hebrew with Sesame Street.*
Minneapolis: Lerner Publications, 2020.

INDEX

Photo Acknowledgments

Image credits: Dana Friedlander for the Israeli Ministry of Tourism/flickr (CC BY-ND 2.0), p. 5; Laura Westlund/Independent Picture Service, pp. 6–7, 21; Dafna Tal for the Israeli Ministry of Tourism/flickr (CC BY-ND 2.0), p. 8; Oleg Zaslavsky/Shutterstock.com, p. 9; Kyrylo Glivin/Shutterstock.com, p. 10; John R. Kreul/Independent Picture Service, p. 11; hermitis/Shutterstock.com, p. 12; arka38/Shutterstock.com, p. 13; Rafael Ben-Ari/Alamy Stock Photo, p. 14 (top); ChameleonsEye/Shutterstock.com, p. 14 (bottom); Nancy Anderson/Shutterstock.com, p. 16; Inna Reznik/Shutterstock.com, p. 17; Nir Alon/Alamy Stock Photo, p. 18; Itamar Grinberg for the Israeli Ministry of Tourism/flickr (CC BY-ND 2.0), p. 20.

Cover: joe daniel price/Moment/Getty Images (top); badahos/Shutterstock.com (bottom).

Lerner Publications Company
An imprint of Lerner Publishing Group, Inc.
241 First Avenue North
Minneapolis, MN 55401 USA

For reading levels and more information, look up this title at www.lernerbooks.com.

Main body text set in Mikado a Regular.
Typeface provided by HVD Fonts.

Lerner team: Martha Kranes

Library of Congress Cataloging-in-Publication Data

Names: Peterson, Christy, author.
Title: Welcome to Israel with Sesame Street / Christy Peterson.
Description: Minneapolis, MN : Lerner Publications, 2022 | Series: Sesame Street friends around the world | Includes bibliographical references and index. | Audience: Ages 4–8 | Audience: Grades K–1 | Summary: "People have lived in Israel for thousands of years. With help from Sesame Street, find out what Israeli families like to eat, how they spend time together, and more about daily life in the desert"— Provided by publisher.
Identifiers: LCCN 2020040847 (print) | LCCN 2020040848 (ebook) | ISBN 9781728424415 (library binding) | ISBN 9781728430515 (ebook)
Subjects: LCSH: Israel—Social life and customs—Juvenile literature.
Classification: LCC DS112 .P48 2021 (print) | LCC DS112 (ebook) | DDC 956.94—dc23

LC record available at https://lccn.loc.gov/2020040847
LC ebook record available at https://lccn.loc.gov/2020040848

Manufactured in the United States of America
1-49311-49427-1/27/2021